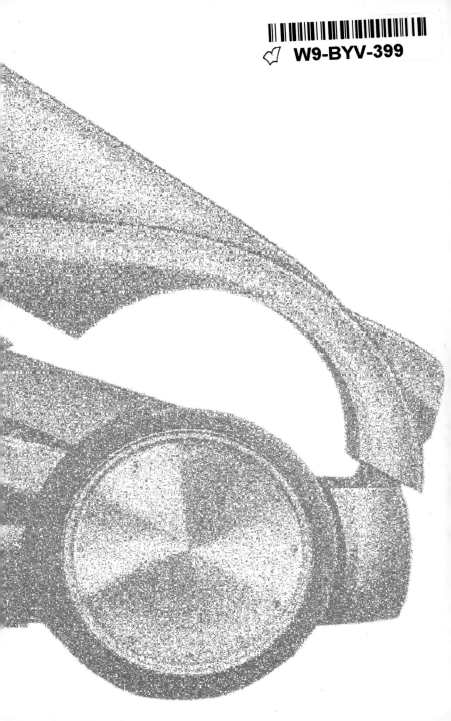

FAST AND COOL CARS

By Leon Gray

Series Editor Deborah Lock
US Senior Editor Shannon Beatty
Project Editor Caryn Jenner
Editor Nandini Gupta
Senior Art Editor Ann Cannings
Art Editor Rashika Kachroo
Managing Editor Soma B. Chowdhury
Managing Art Editor Ahlawat Gunjan
Art Director Martin Wilson
Producer, Pre-production Francesca Wardell
DTP Designers Anita Yadav, Vijay Kandwal
Picture Researcher Sakshi Saluja

Subject Consultant Giles Chapman
Reading Consultant Dr. Linda Gambrell, Ph.D.

First American Edition, 2015
Published in the United States by DK Publishing
345 Hudson Street, New York, New York 10014

Copyright © 2015 Dorling Kindersley Limited
A Penguin Random House Company
15 16 17 18 19 10 9 8 7 6 5 4 3 2 1
001—273358—September/2015

A catalog record for this book is available from the Library of Congress.
ISBN: 978-1-4654-2936-0 (pb)
ISBN: 978-1-4654-2935-3 (hc)

DK books are available at special discounts when purchased
in bulk for sales promotions, premiums, fund-raising, or
educational use. For details, contact: DK Publishing Special
Markets, 345 Hudson Street, New York, New York 10014
SpecialSales@dk.com.

Printed and bound in China

The publisher would like to thank the following for their kind permission to reproduce their photographs:
(Key: a-above; b-below/bottom; c-center; f-far; l-left; r-right; t-top)
1 Dreamstime.com: Pavlos Rekas. **18 Dorling Kindersley:** National Motor Museum, Beaulieu (clb).
19 Alamy Images: Jim West (br). **Getty Images:** Klemantaski Collection (cl). **9 Dorling Kindersley:** R. Florio (b).
10–11 Dorling Kindersley: R. Florio (b). **14–15 Dreamstime.com:** Pavel Losevsky. **21 Dreamstime.com:** Andrey
Armyagov **37 Corbis:** Whisson / Jordan. **38–39 Dorling Kindersley:** Eagle E Types. **49 Corbis:** Jaak Nilson / Spaces
Images **52–53 Dorling Kindersley:** Courtesy of Gilbert and Anna East. **54–55 Dreamstime.com:** Buschmen.
56–57 Dorling Kindersley: Dave Stone (c). **58–59 Dorling Kindersley:** Neil Mort, Mott Motorcycles (t). **60–61 Dorling
Kindersley:** Trevor Pope Motorcycles. **66 Dorling Kindersley:** Scootopia (c); Dave Stone (b). **67 Dorling Kindersley:**
Neil Mort, Mott Motorcycles (b). **Dreamstime.com:** Buschmen (c). **70–71 BMW Group:** (b). **78–79 Fotolia:**
JustContributor. **80–81 Getty Images:** altrendo images / Stockbyte. **82–83 Dreamstime.com:** Aprescindere. **88–89 Corbis:**
Christoph Schmidt / epa (b). **96 Science Photo Library:** Carlos Clarivan. **98 Corbis:** Toyota (GB) PLC: (c). **99 Audi
AG:** (c). **Dreamstime.com:** Yali Shi (t). **102–103 Dreamstime.com:** Monika Wisniewska. **107 Corbis:** Ken Redding.
108–109 Alamy Images: Alvey & Towers Picture Library. **111 Dreamstime.com:** Vladimir Lukovic. **112 Dreamstime.com:**
Laralova (br). **Getty Images:** Onur Döngel / E+ (bl). **113 Dreamstime.com:** Laralova (bc, cr).
Jacket images: Front: Dreamstime.com: Rqs, Maksym Yemelyanov (cb); **Back: Corbis:** Christoph Schmidt / epa (t);
Spine: Getty Images: Simon Wilkinson / Iconica (b)
All other images © Dorling Kindersley
For further information see: www.dkimages.com

A WORLD OF IDEAS:
SEE ALL THERE IS TO KNOW

CONTENTS

4

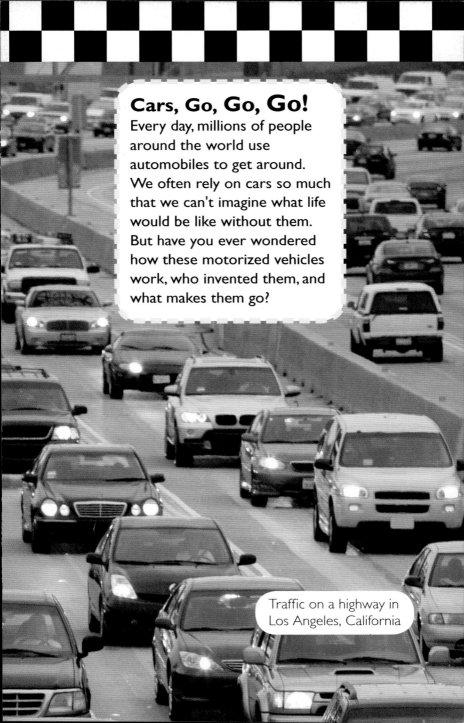

Cars, Go, Go, Go!

Every day, millions of people around the world use automobiles to get around. We often rely on cars so much that we can't imagine what life would be like without them. But have you ever wondered how these motorized vehicles work, who invented them, and what makes them go?

Traffic on a highway in Los Angeles, California

CHAPTER 1
Cars for Everyone

For more than 5,000 years, horses were the main form of transportation. Then cars were invented in the late 1800s, and the world of transportation changed. In the earliest days of motoring, automobiles were expensive and only very wealthy people could afford cars. From the beginning of the 20th century, cars became cheaper as more and more manufacturers started mass producing cars. Car culture swept across the developing world, and driving became a convenient way to get around.

Early Cars

In 1893, German engineer Karl Benz made the first four-wheeled car, the Benz Victoria, followed by the Benz Velo. Benz's range of cars was popular and, by the start of the 20th century, his company was one of the world's leading car manufacturers.

Other engineers followed, such as the Renault brothers from France, Charles Rolls and Henry Royce from Britain, and Ransom E. Olds from the United States.

However, early cars were unreliable and once the car got going, driving could be dangerous. There were no rules of the road and drivers didn't need a license. Crashes were common.

Improvements

Automobiles gradually became more dependable. Cars were made with sleek aluminum bodies and smoother, quieter engines. Manufacturers added spring **suspension** and air-filled (pneumatic) rubber tires to make driving more comfortable. Many motor cars had luxurious, hand-built interiors using expensive materials such as leather and velvet. Mudguards protected the driver and passengers from spray thrown up from the wheels. Manufacturers started to think about safety, adding height to the driving seat to give the driver a clear view of the road ahead. Cars were fitted with headlights for visibility when driving in the dark. Drivers could also sound a horn to warn any pedestrians who strayed onto the road.

In these early days, driving was an expensive way to travel. Teams of mechanics made the parts by hand and assembled each car one at a time. As a result, only the very wealthy could afford to buy a car. All that changed in 1908, when a young pioneering American manufacturer called Henry Ford set up a factory to build his Model T Ford cars in Michigan in the United States. Ford revolutionized automobile manufacture using a technique called mass production.

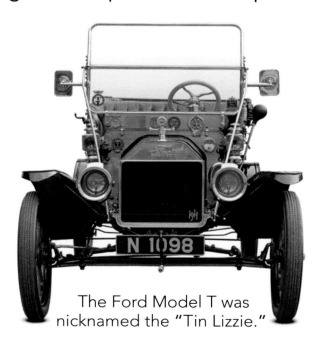

The Ford Model T was nicknamed the "Tin Lizzie."

Mass Production

Ford hired lots of mechanics at his factory and set up a production line. Each Model T Ford moved along the line, where each mechanic did just one job, such as fitting the wheels or spraying the bodywork. When the mechanic finished, the car moved along to the next mechanic, who did a different job. In this way, Ford's production line could churn out one car every three minutes—each taking less than one hour to assemble.

Ford Model T with an open folding roof visible at the back

One key to Ford's success was his use of a standard car body. Most other automobile manufacturers built cars to order, which made them very expensive. Ford offered a limited range of models, but the chassis was always the same, so it was easier to manufacture different models on the same production line.

Ford's cars were cheaper than those of his rivals. Car ownership became a reality for lots of people, not just the wealthy. In 1908, when Ford started mass producing Model T Fords, about 200,000 people owned a car in the United States. Within five years, more than 250,000 people owned a Model T Ford, and by 1924, Ford's factories had built and sold more than 10 million of these cars.

Car Culture

The time between the 1920s and 1960s could be described as the "golden age of motoring." Many new manufacturers started building cars and engineers made improvements to their design and technology. People loved this emerging "car culture." What better way to spend the weekend than take a picnic and head out on the open road or go to the local drive-in movie theater?

Manufacturers expanded production to make and sell different types of cars for different people.

Four-door sedans such as the Austin Ten were popular family cars, while wealthy car enthusiasts focused on performance cars with powerful engines, such as Alfa Romeo and Aston Martin. These high-end models were built on the success of racing cars, and the technology that pushed them to victory on the racetrack was soon being used in cars sold for everyday motoring. One example is the **supercharger**, which gave an extra burst of speed by increasing the amount of air delivered to the engine.

1965 Aston Martin DB5

Improved Roads

Roads also began to improve. Throughout the first half of the 20th century, dusty trails were replaced with smooth tarmac, and multi-lane highways opened up between major city centers. These expanded road networks meant that people could travel greater distances. Traffic control measures such as traffic lights, speed limits, and road signs were introduced. Electric lighting illuminated roads at night so people could drive their cars in the dark.

Modern Car Manufacture

Today's motor car technology is firmly rooted in computer control. Cars are still made on production lines, but robots have replaced human mechanics for assembling the basic frame more quickly and efficiently. Modern cars have computers that control everything from fuel consumption to engine **efficiency**. In the future, computers may even drive the car, using global positioning satellites (GPS) to find the way and sensors to keep a safe distance from other cars on the road.

Classic Modern Car

The 2004 Morgan Roadster may look old, but its powerful engine can reach a top speed of 134 mph (215 km/h). Unlike most modern cars, the Morgan Roadster is built by hand, using traditional skills.

MORGAN

TIMELINE OF
FAST, COOL CARS AND BIKES

1800s

1860s French engineer builds the first steam-powered car with an **internal combustion** engine.

1877 German engineer Nikolaus Otto demonstrates the four-stroke internal combustion engine.

1885 German engineer Karl Benz sells a gasoline-powered three-wheel car called the Benz Patent-Motorwagen.

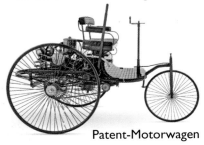
Patent-Motorwagen

1885 German engineer Gottlieb Daimler uses a gas engine to build the first motorcycle. It has a wooden frame and a top speed of 12 mph (19km/h).

1894 German company Hildebrand & Wolfmüller sells the world's first mass-produced motorcycle.

1895 Charles and Fran Duryea found the Duryea Motor Wagon Company—the first American carmaker.

1898 Frenchman Comte Gaston de Chasseloup-Laubat sets the first land speed record in a Jeantaud electric car traveling at 39 mph (63 km/h).

1900s

1903 Harley-Davidson starts to produce motorcycles in America.

1908 American engineer Henry Ford introduces the mass-produced Model T car in America. Over 1.3 million Model T cars were produced in 1923.

1932 Ford introduces the compact V8 engine.

1938 German carmaker Volkswagen launches the VW "Beetle."

1946 Italian company Piaggio introduces the Vespa scooter.

1947 Enzo Ferrari founds the Ferrari automobile company with the 125 Sport race car.

1948 William France establishes the NASCAR racing series in America.

1950 The first World Drivers' Formula 1 Championship at Silverstone, England, is won by Italian Giuseppe Farina in his Alfa Romeo 159.

Giuseppe Farina

1953 General Motors unveils the first American mass-produced sportscar—the Corvette.

1954 Mercedes-Benz releases the 300SL—the first car with fuel injection as standard for high performance.

1959 Honda becomes the world's biggest motorcycle manufacturer.

1966 Toyota releases the Corolla—one of the best-selling cars of all time.

1997 Toyota releases the Prius, the world's most popular hybrid electric car.

2000s

2010 Nissan launches the electric car known as the Leaf.

2011 Three identical Mercedes-Benz B-Class F-CELL hydrogen **fuel-cell** cars circumnavigate the world in 125 days.

2014 Ford reveals the C-MAX Solar Energi Concept Car powered by solar panels on the roof.

Ford Solar Energi Concept Car

CHAPTER 2
Car Design

Many different people contribute to the creation of a new car. Design engineers and production engineers use their skills to develop a style of car that people will want to buy and drive.

Research and Development

Before a new model is released for sale, car manufacturers research the market to find out what drivers want. Designers work out their ideas using paper sketches and wireframe images to full-size clay models and working **prototypes**. It's a long process.

From these sketches and models, industrial designers make detailed technical drawings using computer-aided design (CAD). CAD programs not only show the final shape of the car, they also allow manufacturers to make changes to the design—often at the touch of a button.

The Prototype

Once the design is set, the manufacturer builds a prototype—a full-size model of the car that lets the manufacturer see how all the different parts of the car fit together. The prototype can then be tested for safety, comfort, roadholding, engine response, and overall performance.

Modern Motoring

Today, car manufacturing is dominated by computer technology. While the designs vary, all modern cars have computer-controlled engines that monitor performance and keep the car working with maximum efficiency.

Sensors detect information such as how much fuel and air is sucked into the engine and what the temperature is inside the car. This information is fed back to the computer to make continual adjustments to the running of the car. The onboard computer also controls features such as the airbag and the anti-lock braking systems (ABS) to ensure the safety of the driver and passengers.

The computer can even detect if something is wrong, and flashes an engine warning light. Mechanics can then download error codes from the computer to assess what needs to be fixed.

What is ABS the abbreviation for?

Interior Design

Car designers must consider every aspect of the car, from the engine to the upholstery to the design of the dashboard, steering column, and gear stick. This Morgan Aero 8 has a distinctive aluminum dashboard.

Cars, Cars, and More Cars

By 2014, the number of vehicles driving on the world's roads was more than one billion. While many older cars are scrapped, more than 50 million new cars are added every year. The huge number of cars on the road is using up a lot of fuel and contributing to the problems of air **pollution** and city center congestion.

As a result, manufacturers are making cars with engines that create less pollution. Computer controls help cut down these exhaust **emissions**. Smart sensors in the car's engine control unit constantly monitor the fuel consumption to ensure that emissions are kept within an acceptable range.

Modern cars are also built with streamlined, or aerodynamic, shapes. A car has to punch through the air as it goes forward, but drag is the force of the air rushing past that holds the car back. During the design process, the shape of the car is tested in a wind tunnel to ensure that the car will cut through the air with minimum drag, or air resistance. Air collides with the sharp corners of box-shaped cars, creating a mess of disturbed swirls. Smooth, long, low cars push a smaller hole through the air, allowing the air to flow more easily over the top. This means the engine needs less power to move, so it uses less fuel and is more efficient.

Car manufacturers also continue to be challenged to develop new ways to power cars.

Approximately how many new cars are added to the roads every year?

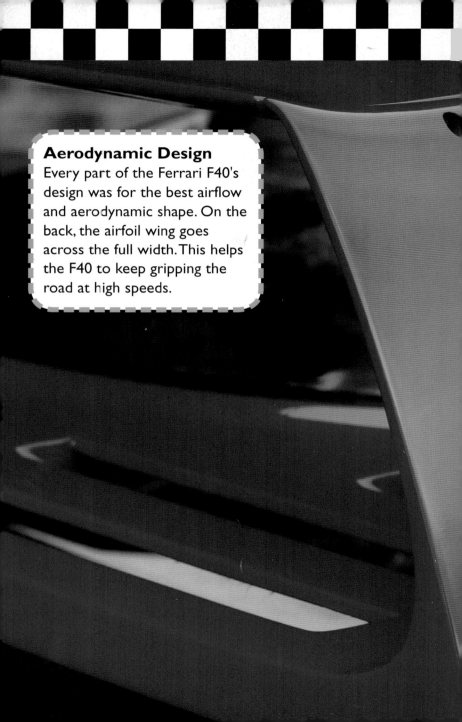

Aerodynamic Design

Every part of the Ferrari F40's design was for the best airflow and aerodynamic shape. On the back, the airfoil wing goes across the full width. This helps the F40 to keep gripping the road at high speeds.

CHAPTER 3
Car Engines

In the 1700s, engineers in Britain had harnessed the power of steam to turn the wheels of steam locomotives. These steam engines burned coal in a furnace, using the heat from the fire to boil water and make steam. The steam drove pistons connected to the wheels of the locomotive to make it move. In 1769, French mechanic Nicolas Cugnot used a steam engine to power a tractor. This was the first self-propelled road vehicle.

By the middle of the 1800s, steam engines were ideal for big locomotives traveling on rails, but they were far from ideal for powering smaller vehicles running on roads. Companies such as Stanley, White, and Locomobile as well as individual inventors were developing steam-powered carriages. However, these were heavy and slow, and choked the air with black smoke.

A New Engine

In 1869, a Belgian engineer called Etienne Lenoir invented a new type of engine that burned coal gas inside a metal engine. This was the first internal combustion engine. "Combustion" means burning, and the internal combustion engine was so named because it burned coal gas inside **cylinders** in the engine rather than burning the fuel in an open fire.

The invention of the internal combustion engine marked the beginning of the history of the modern automobile. Lenoir's engine was small, but powerful enough to drive a vehicle on the road.

A few years later, German engineer Nikolaus Otto designed a more efficient internal combustion engine. With the help of fellow engineer Gottlieb Daimler, Otto also adapted it to burn gasoline instead of coal gas. Otto's engine design is the basis for almost all modern automobile engines.

Inside the Engine

An internal combustion engine converts the energy locked away inside gasoline into the movement of the car's wheels. The engine unlocks this energy by burning the gasoline inside small metal chambers called cylinders.

The cylinders are tubes cut into a lump of metal called the cylinder block. A car engine can have up to 16 cylinders in the cylinder block.

When the driver turns the key in the ignition, an electric spark ignites a mixture of fuel and air inside each cylinder. The fuel-air mixture explodes, and the explosion drives pistons up and down inside each cylinder. The up-and-down movement of the pistons drives a metal rod called a **crankshaft**, which turns the wheels of the automobile.

What invention marked the beginning of the history of the modern automobile?

An internal combustion engine converts energy from the gasoline into movement of the car's wheels. The engine description indicates the number of cylinders. For example, a V6 engine has 6 cylinders. Fuel and air explode to drive the pistons in the cylinders up and down. For each explosion, the piston moves four times. This is a **four-stroke cycle.**

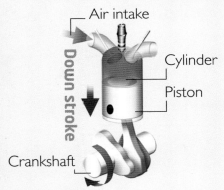

Air intake

Down stroke

Cylinder

Piston

Crankshaft

Up stroke

1. Intake As the piston moves down, the cylinder takes in air. At the same time, the fuel injector squirts a tiny amount of gas into the cylinder.

2. Compression The piston moves up the cylinder, squeezing the fuel-air mixture together.

The Pistons and Crankshaft

A crankshaft converts the up-and-down movement of all the pistons into the circular movement of the wheels. Just think of your legs as the pistons the next time you ride your bike!

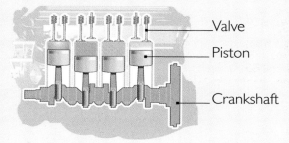

Valve

Piston

Crankshaft

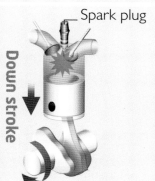

Spark plug

Down stroke

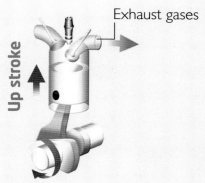

Exhaust gases

Up stroke

3. Explosion As the piston reaches the top, a spark from the spark plug ignites the fuel-air mixture, driving the piston back down the cylinder.

4. Exhaust The piston moves back up the cylinder, forcing burned gases into the car's exhaust system.

Engine Power

German engineer Karl Benz made the first practical motorized vehicle in 1886. His vehicle, called the "Benz Patent-Motorwagen," was powered by a single cylinder four-stroke internal combustion engine. It could reach a top speed of 10 miles (16 km) per hour.

Modern automobiles are now much more powerful. Engines are much bigger and have more cylinders to burn more gasoline. The pistons also move much faster. The cylinders in a car engine can be arranged in a straight line or in rows to make a V-shape. Most family cars have four cylinders in a straight line, while speedy sports cars may have six, eight, or even twelve cylinders in a V-shape. The V-shape keeps the engine compact and well balanced. These cars can be very noisy and very powerful.

High-performance cars often have

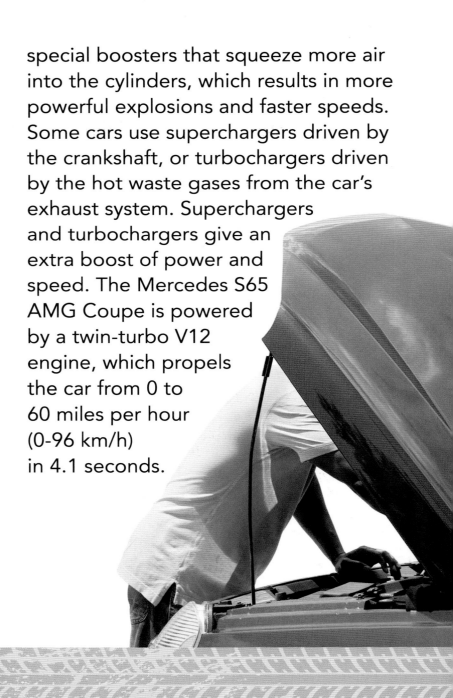

special boosters that squeeze more air into the cylinders, which results in more powerful explosions and faster speeds. Some cars use superchargers driven by the crankshaft, or turbochargers driven by the hot waste gases from the car's exhaust system. Superchargers and turbochargers give an extra boost of power and speed. The Mercedes S65 AMG Coupe is powered by a twin-turbo V12 engine, which propels the car from 0 to 60 miles per hour (0-96 km/h) in 4.1 seconds.

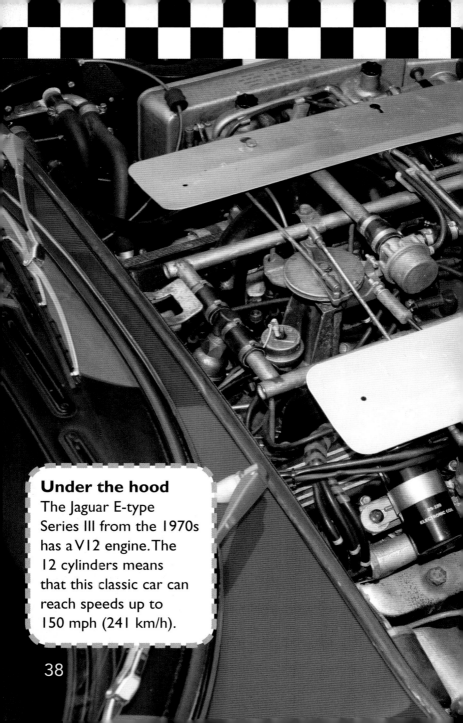

Under the hood
The Jaguar E-type Series III from the 1970s has a V12 engine. The 12 cylinders means that this classic car can reach speeds up to 150 mph (241 km/h).

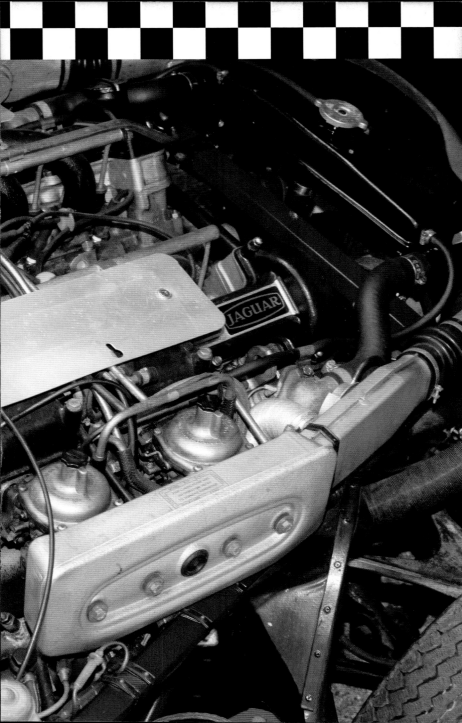

In Gear

The crankshaft is the part of the engine that converts the up-and-down movement of the pistons into the turning force of the wheels. This turning force is called torque. Traveling along a level road at constant speed may not require much torque, but you need more torque to accelerate along the road or drive up a steep hill.

Cars use gears to increase the torque that is produced by the engine. The gears in a car are metal cogs of different sizes that line up inside the gearbox. The cogs have teeth that interlock with other cogs to handle different driving conditions.

To get a car moving or to climb a steep hill, a low gear is used. The wheels of the car will move slowly but with lots of torque. To cruise along a highway, a high gear is used. The wheels of the car will move much quicker but with less torque.

Slowing Down

Cars need a way to slow down as well as speed up. To slow down, the driver pushes his or her foot down on the brake pedal. This pedal is connected to the brakes on each wheel via fluid-filled pipes. When the driver steps on the brake pedal, the force of the foot is transmitted through the fluid in the brake pipes to brake pads at each wheel. The pads clamp hard against the brake disk on the wheel. The rubbing between the pad and the disk slows the wheel and reduces the speed of the car.

Would you use a high gear or low gear to get a car moving or to climb a steep hill? Does this gear use lots of torque or a little?

Diesel Power

Some car engines use a type of fuel called diesel instead of gasoline. Diesel engines do not need a spark plug to ignite the diesel and air inside the cylinders. Instead, the fuel and air explode spontaneously when the piston squeezes the mixture during the compression stroke. Diesel contains more energy than gasoline, so diesel cars can travel a greater distance for the same amount of fuel. The Porsche Panamera Diesel can travel 44.1 miles (71 km) per gallon.

However, diesel produces more harmful emissions when it burns, so most diesel engines are worse for the environment than gasoline ones.

What are some advantages and disadvantages of diesel-powered cars?

Diesel engine

43

CHAPTER 4
Guzzling Gas

Gasoline is the fuel used for most modern motor vehicles. This energy-rich liquid comes from crude oil, the fossilized remains of plants and animals that lived millions of years ago. Deposits of crude oil are buried deep under the ground or beneath the ocean floor. Every year, oil companies spend billions of dollars finding new sources of crude oil to supply the world with the fuel that people want.

Fossil Fuel

The gasoline we use as a fuel for cars and other motor vehicles is a **fossil fuel**. Millions of years ago, the world's oceans were teeming with tiny sea plants and animals called plankton. The plankton floated near the surface of the water, soaking up energy from the Sun and using it to make food.

In turn, most plankton became food for fish and other sea creatures. Plankton that was not eaten died and settled as a layer of sludge on the ocean floor.

Over millions of years, layer upon layer of mud and sand trapped the plankton sludge under the seabed. The huge pressure of the layers above changed the sludge into crude oil. Today, oil companies drill deep under the ground or beneath the ocean floor to find these deposits of crude oil.

Gasoline makes up 45 percent of crude oil.
There is a limited amount of crude oil on
our planet. It has been used for over 5,000
years. Once it's gone, there will be no more
fuel to power our gas-powered vehicles.

Crude oil

Oil is measured in barrels, which is
equal to 42 US gallons (159 liters).
The US uses more oil than any
other country—nearly 19 million
barrels every day.

Oil drilling begins with
a drill cutting through
the Earth. Air is pumped
downward, so that once
the oil is hit, the air forces
the oil to rush to the
surface, shooting hundreds
of feet out of the ground.

Drilling rig

Crude oil

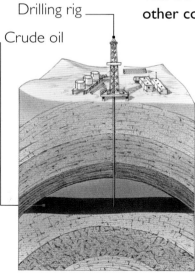

46

The process to make crude oil took millions of years. The crude oil produced is also known as a "fossil" fuel because it came from fossils. We use fossil fuels for power. The problem is that there is a limited supply buried under the ground.

Oil reserves can be found all over the world. The US has the 12th largest oil reserve in the world, with an estimated 30 billion barrels. Venezuela and Saudi Arabia have the largest, each with more than 200 billion barrels. Every year, this number decreases.

Fuel for thought

Oil wells drill deep down into the ground to extract the oil trapped between layers of rock.

Problems with Fossil Fuels

According to the International Energy Agency, the world's daily consumption of crude oil could rise from 89 million barrels in 2011 to more than 115 million barrels by 2030. However, there is only a limited amount of crude oil on the planet. Scientists estimate that the world could run out of fossil fuels by the end of this century.

Another problem is pollution caused by burning fossil fuels. Exhaust gases from automobiles include carbon dioxide and nitrogen gases. Carbon dioxide traps heat in Earth's atmosphere and contributes to climate change—the gradual human-made increase in Earth's temperature. Nitrogen gases such as nitrous oxides are one of the main causes of acid rain. As the rain falls back down on Earth, it increases the acidity of lakes and oceans, killing fish and other marine animals and plants.

In addition to these problems, there have also been major oil spills that have leaked millions of gallons of oil into the ocean. Accidents such as these have a devastating effect on marine life and the environment.

Vehicle drivers fill fuel tanks at a gas station.

Fuels of the Future

Automobile manufacturers are investigating alternative sources of fuel to power motor vehicles. "Alternative fuel vehicles" refers to any vehicle that does not rely on fossil fuels alone for power. These include hybrid cars, which use a combination of gasoline and electricity, and hydrogen cars, which use fuel cells to generate electricity for power.

Biofuels

Another development are biofuels, which are fuels produced from plant material. Biofuels include biodiesel, made from the oils of rapeseed and other plants, as well as bioethanol, made by fermenting sugarcane and wheat. Unlike fossil fuels, biofuels are a renewable source of fuel, so they can be produced as they are needed.

Many manufacturers including Audi, Ford, and Volvo build vehicles that can run on biofuels and work with suppliers.

However, many people are concerned that biofuels might use up plants that could otherwise feed hungry people around the world. Although biofuels would reduce our reliance on the limited supply of fossil fuels, is it worth it? There are no easy answers.

Name some examples of "alternative fuel vehicles."

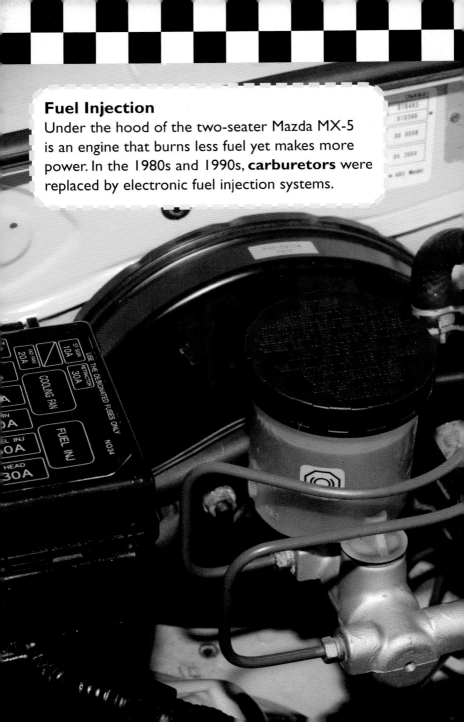

Fuel Injection

Under the hood of the two-seater Mazda MX-5 is an engine that burns less fuel yet makes more power. In the 1980s and 1990s, **carburetors** were replaced by electronic fuel injection systems.

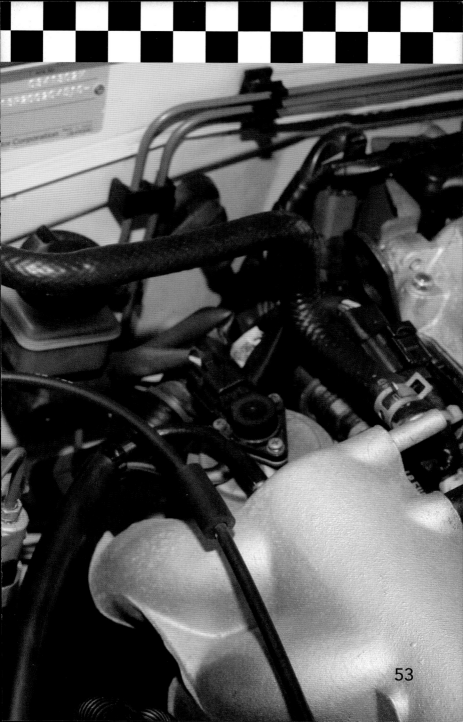

53

CHAPTER 5
Motorcycles

Motorcycles are a popular alternative to cars. These gasoline-powered vehicles combine the speed of a motor car with the adventure and freedom of a pedal-powered bicycle. Motorcycles were developed in Europe soon after the invention of the internal combustion engine in the late 19th century. Since then, the manufacturing of motorcycles has spread throughout the world. In many developing countries, motorcycles are the main form of transportation because people cannot afford cars.

Honda XL250 Enduro

Motorcycle History

In1885, Gottlieb Daimler, made the first two-wheeled motorcycle. It was called the Petroleum Reitwagen and it could reach a top speed of 7 miles (11 km) per hour.

As engineers improved the design of gasoline engines, the motorcycle

Harley-Davidson "Fat Boy"

industry flourished, with companies such as Triumph in Britain and Harley-Davidson in the United States. Both of these companies are still making motorcycles today, although the high-speed performance models made by Japanese manufacturers such as Honda, Suzuki, and Yamaha are also very popular.

Motorcycle Engine

The basic design of the motorcycle has changed very little since the early 20th century. Like motor cars, motorcycles are powered by an internal combustion engine. The engine converts the up-and-down movement of pistons into the turning motion of the back

Triumph Sprint ST050 ABS

wheel of the motorcycle. Motorcycles can have up to six cylinders in the block, but most have two cylinder engines, which can be arranged in a straight line or in a V-shape.

The **transmission** of power from the engine to the back wheel occurs in one of three ways. The most common transmission is through a chain. This chain connects a small toothed wheel near the engine, called a sprocket, to a larger rear sprocket mounted on the back wheel. Other transmission systems use belt drives made from tough rubber or even heavy metal drive shafts.

Motorcycle engines are measured in cubic centimeters (cc) and can be between 50cc for scooters and mopeds to 1,800cc for high-performance racing and touring bikes.

Exhaust

Chain

Clutch cover

Engine

Brake pedal

Sprocket

This Suzuki RM-Z 450 has a 449cc engine.

Drive system

The drive system in most motorcycles consists of
a chain attached to the rear wheel. The chain drives a
small, toothed wheel called a sprocket. In turn, this
drives a larger sprocket connected to the rear wheel.
It works in a similar way to the chain and
sprockets on your bicycle!

Motorcycle gears

A motorcycle engine delivers
an enormous amount of
power to the wheels through
the gears and drive system.
The gears control the
power, so the rider can
move from a standing
start to cruising speed
in a controllable way.
The clutch allows the
rider to change
through the gears.

61

Motorcycle Chassis

The chassis is the structure of the motorcycle that holds all the different parts together. The chassis consists of a lightweight metal or metal alloy frame that connects the engine, wheels, and suspension.

Suspension System

Motorcycles also have a suspension system to absorb bumpy roads or trails. The suspension system has springs and shock absorbers that keep the wheels on the ground and smooth out the ride.

Brakes

To stop the motorcycle, the rider pulls on a brake lever on the right side of the handlebars to slow the front wheel. The rider operates the rear brake by pushing down on a pedal with the right foot. The brakes work in much the same way as the brakes of a car, with brake pads squeezing against a disk on each wheel.

Wheels

The wheels are usually made of aluminum or steel and have rubber air-filled (pneumatic) tires. The tires can be smooth with incredible grip for riding on smooth roads, or rough and knobbly for off-road riding.

Riding a Motorcycle

Riding a motorcycle is very different from driving a car. New riders must learn motorcycling skills and take a test to get a motorcycle license. One main cause of motorcycle accidents is riders locking the rear brake and skidding. When a rider slows down, all the weight of the motorcycle is transferred to the front wheel. This can make the rear wheel lock up and skid. Car drivers must also take extra care to look out for people on motorcycles.

Motorcycles Around the World

Motorcycles have become very popular in many different parts of the world. Low-power motorcycles such as mopeds and scooters are much more affordable than cars. They remain the best way to get around in congested city centers, particularly in Asia. In other

Motorcycle riders in Bali, Indonesia

parts of the world, such as Europe and the United States, motorcycle enthusiasts belong to clubs and ride together for fun. Others have developed an entire "biker culture" made popular in TV programs and movies. Today, there are many different types of motorcycles, from high-performance sports bikes and large touring machines to dirt bikes and traditional cruisers.

Classic Motorcycles

DUCATI M900 MONSTER

TOP SPEED: 130 mph (209 km/h)   **0–60 mph (0–96 km/h):** 3.9 seconds

ENGINE CAPACITY: 904cc   **WEIGHT:** 417 lbs (189 kg)

VESPA SCOOTER

TOP SPEED: 55 mph (89 km/h)   **0–60 mph (0–96 km/h):** 8.1 seconds

ENGINE CAPACITY: 125 cc   **WEIGHT:** 172 lbs (78 kg)

HARLEY-DAVIDSON "FAT BOY"

TOP SPEED: 110 mph (177 km/h)   **0–60 mph (0–96 km/h):** 5.8 seconds

ENGINE CAPACITY: 1,449 cc   **WEIGHT:** 705 lbs (320 kg)

SUNBEAM

TOP SPEED: 70 mph (113 km/h)   **0–60 mph (0–96 km/h):** Not known

ENGINE CAPACITY: 492 cc   **WEIGHT:** 238 lbs (108 kg)

HONDA XL250

TOP SPEED: 71 mph (114 km/h)   **0–60 mph (0–96 km/h):** 11.7 seconds

ENGINE CAPACITY: 250 cc   **WEIGHT:** 291 lbs (132 kg)

TRIUMPH SPRINT ST050 ABS

TOP SPEED: 160 mph (258 km/h)   **0–60 mph (0–96 km/h):** 2.8 seconds

ENGINE CAPACITY: 1,050 cc   **WEIGHT:** 463 lbs (210 kg)

CHAPTER 6

Hybrid Cars

Today, not all cars run purely on gasoline. One of the main developments is hybrid cars, which use a combination of gasoline and electricity to power modern cars. The word "hybrid" refers to the combination of two fuels.

Dual-Fuel Vehicles

The idea of a hybrid vehicle is not a new one. Mopeds (motorized pedal bikes) are hybrid vehicles because they combine gasoline engines with pedal power to drive them. Many locomotives that pull trains are also hybrids, relying on a combination of diesel and electricity for power.

Hybrid cars are a real alternative to the gas-guzzling automobiles people are used to driving. Most car manufacturers either currently make or have plans to make hybrid models, such as Toyota's Prius and the Honda Civic Hybrid.

Conventional Gas Engine

Most commercial hybrid cars run on a combination of gasoline and electricity. Cars powered by gasoline have an internal combustion engine. The engine burns the gas stored in a fuel tank to drive the transmission, which then turns the wheels of the car. Hybrids have an internal combustion engine that works in exactly the same way.

Electric Power

Hybrid cars can also use electricity from **batteries** to power an **electric motor**. The motor works using complex electronics. It draws electricity from the batteries to drive the transmission and turn the wheels of the car.

Hybrid cars generally use a combination of which two types of fuel?

BMW i8 hybrid car

How a Hybrid Works

At low speeds, hybrid cars rely only on the electric motor for power. When accelerating or climbing a hill, the internal combustion engine and electric motor work together. When the driver steps on the brakes to slow the car, the electric motor generates electricity, recharging the batteries while driving. In addition, the motor provides the electrical spark to start the internal combustion engine, eliminating the need for a separate starter motor.

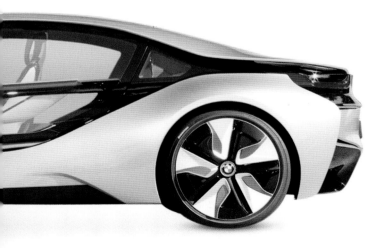

Fuel efficient! 100% torque from standstill!
Charge up batteries on the go! Save energy!
Hybrid cars combine the clean pulling power
and quick pick-up of an electric motor with
the long range of a gasoline-powered engine.
Features include an on-board generator and
regenerative braking to make electricity.
Could hybrid supercars save the planet?

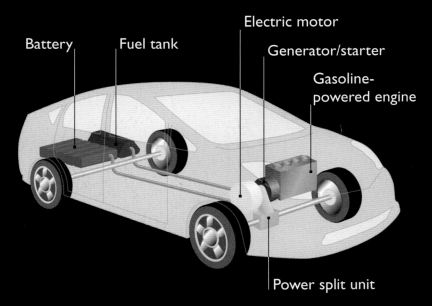

Electric motor

Battery

Fuel tank

Generator/starter

Gasoline-
powered engine

Power split unit

GASOLINE + ELECTRICS = HYBRID

The gasoline-powered engine and electric motor are combined to fit the driving conditions. The driver doesn't notice the difference.

 **Electric**

The car starts using the battery-charged electric motor.

 **Gas**

The gas-powered engine is used for normal driving.

  **Gas + electric**

Both the gas engine and the electric motor are used to accelerate, or go faster.

  **Battery recharging**

The battery recharges when the car decelerates, for example, to go down hills.

 **Electric**

The electric motor is used in stop-start conditions, for example, in a traffic jam.

73

Hybrid Advantages

The combination of gasoline and electric power increases the mileage of hybrid cars while also reducing the harmful emissions produced by standard gas-powered cars. These cars are usually made of a lightweight material such as aluminum. A lighter car means that the internal combustion engine can be smaller and lighter, making the hybrid car more efficient.

Regenerative Braking

The electric motor supplies power when the hybrid accelerates, and also generates electricity when it slows down. This is called regenerative braking. When the driver applies the brakes, the car loses energy in the form of heat. The electric motor in the hybrid traps some of this wasted energy while slowing the vehicle down. The motor acts like a generator, converting the heat energy into electrical energy. This electricity can then be stored in the battery to use later. Some "plug-in" hybrid cars can also be plugged into an electrical outlet to recharge the batteries, as well as being charged on the move.

Aerodynamics

Cars lose a lot of energy through drag force, which is the airstream colliding with the wheels and body of the car as it speeds along the highway. Automobile manufacturers design hybrids with aerodynamics in mind. Most hybrid cars have streamlined "teardrop" shapes that cut through the air with minimum drag force. They also use low-rolling resistance tires, which are harder than standard tires. This reduces the rubbing of the tires on the road, improving the efficiency of the car even more.

Electric Cars

Some car manufacturers have built fully electric cars with no internal combustion engine. All the power comes from an electric motor, so these cars are cheap to run and do not pollute the environment with harmful exhaust emissions. The motor also provides amazing acceleration. One electric car—the Tesla Roadster—can accelerate from 0 to 60 miles (96 km) per hour in just four seconds and has a top speed of 125 miles (200 km) per hour.

Despite these impressive features, electric cars have several limitations. The main drawback is their restricted range. Electric cars can only manage around 200 miles (320 km) before the batteries need to be recharged, and the recharging time may take several hours. Another issue is that the motor produces no sound so pedestrians cannot hear them coming. Finally, while electric cars do not produce pollution directly, the electricity they use comes from power stations, which produce electricity by burning fossil fuels.

Hybrids of the Future

Some of these problems might be solved by another dual-fuel combination being explored by manufacturers—a gasoline engine combined with solar-powered electric batteries. These batteries would be automatically charged by sunlight so they would not need to be recharged at home or some other facility, and wouldn't burn fossil fuels.

How fast can a Tesla Roadster electric car accelerate from 0 to 60 miles (96 km) per hour? What is the Roadster's top speed?

Hybrid Cars

Presenting the next generation of hybrid cars, combining the clean, environmentally friendly power of an electric motor with the reliability and range of a gasoline engine. The hybrid engine switches between gas and electric power to keep the car running as efficiently as possible!

Your highway to the future

Top hybrids

BMW i3 hatchback
range economy: 470 miles (756 km) per gallon
Carbon dioxide emissions: 21 g/mi (13 g/km)

Vauxhall Ampera hatchback
range economy: 200 miles (322 km) per gallon
Carbon dioxide emissions: 43 g/mi (27 g/km)

Volkswagen Golf GTE hatchback
range economy: 188 miles (303 km) per gallon
Carbon dioxide emissions: 56 g/mi (35 g/km)

Save gas, save the planet!

▌ Save money at the gas station. Hybrid cars give you about 30 miles (48 km) extra per gallon of gas than a standard gas-powered car.

▌ Protect the environment. Hybrid cars burn less gas and produce less harmful exhaust emissions.

CHAPTER 7
Solar Power

Imagine a car that runs without the need for expensive fuel that pollutes the environment or even recharging batteries. Solar power may make this dream become a reality.

Energy from the Sun

Most people are familiar with solar power. You might have seen solar panels on roofs of houses or other buildings. These panels trap the energy in sunlight. Special cells inside the panels convert the Sun's energy into electricity. The electricity can then be used to heat and light the home and power electrical appliances such as televisions and washing machines.

Fuel from the Sun

Solar-powered cars may seem like a crazy idea. In fact, all vehicles are powered by solar energy. Fossil fuels such as gasoline and diesel come from the remains of plankton that lived millions of years ago. Like plants, these microscopic living things used the Sun to make food in a process called photosynthesis. When they died, the remains slowly rotted away to form fuel. Gasoline-powered cars rely on the energy trapped inside these fossilized plankton.

The aim of solar-powered cars is to harness the energy of direct sunlight. Unfortunately, it is incredibly difficult to get enough energy from sunlight. Scientists and engineers have steadily improved solar technology to build prototypes of working solar cars.

These vehicles rely on large solar panels, which are made up of units called photovoltaic cells (PVCs). These cells absorb the energy in sunlight and convert it into electricity. Still, they currently work best in very sunny countries such as Australia.

How are all vehicles powered by solar energy?

SOLAR ENERGY

On a bright, sunny day, you can feel the energy in sunlight for yourself. The Sun's energy warms your skin and makes you feel hot. This same energy can be used to generate electricity.

Solar panels

A solar panel consists of individual solar cells made from a material called a **semiconductor**. When the Sun shines on the panel, the semiconductor absorbs the energy from the light. This creates a flow of tiny particles called electrons, which produces an electrical current. If you connect the panels to metal wires, you can draw off the electricity and store it in a battery to be used as a source of power.

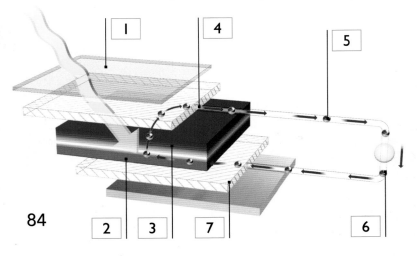

In a solar-powered car, the battery powers an electric motor. This converts electrical energy into the movement of the car's wheels. Solar-powered cars do not produce harmful exhaust emissions. However, solar panels can't always convert all the energy in sunlight into electricity, so solar-powered cars are not very reliable.

Solar cars

1 Sunlight passes through a glass coating.

2 Light gives up its energy to electrons in the bottom layer (blue).

3 Electrons use energy to jump to top layer (red).

4 Contact layer receives electrons, then passes them to the outside circuit.

5 Electrons flow around the circuit.

6 Movement of electrons provides electrical power.

7 Electrons reenter bottom contact layer.

Solar facts

✳ Australian racing driver Barton Mawer set the land speed record for a solar-powered car in 2011. The Sunswift IV, designed by students at the University of New South Wales, reached 55 miles an hour (89 km/h).

✳ Solar panels are often used to supply power for satellites and spacecraft operating in outer space!

Solar Technology

Solar vehicles may seem like a new technology, but people have been experimenting since the 1970s. The first solar-powered car was built by Ed Passerini in 1977. He called it the "Bluebird." Since then, many other scientists and engineers have built "concept cars" or experimental designs that aim to push the technology forward.

Some large automobile companies have also tried to make solar power work, including Mazda's Senku from 2005 and Ford's Reflex from 2006. One success story is the Tindo bus, which operates in the city of Adelaide in Australia. The Tindo is not equipped with solar panels, but runs on batteries charged from the solar power generated by panels at the central bus station.

Limitations of solar power

Since the amount of electricity generated by the panels is so small, solar vehicles are not very fast or powerful. Most only have room for one person. The design of solar vehicles must be streamlined to cut through the air. This minimizes the amount of energy lost by drag.

The cars also need to be very lightweight. Engineers have looked at storing electricity in batteries onboard the vehicle but this adds too much weight. There is also the problem of comfort. As you can imagine, sitting in a solar-powered car can get a little hot since the driver must sit under solar cells.

Why aren't solar vehicles very fast or very powerful?

Although the Sun is a free source of energy, solar panels are expensive to make and buy. While the panels are becoming cheaper and more efficient, the biggest  problem in solar technology is the limited lifespan of the panels. Solar panels that generate electricity for houses have a maximum lifespan of 30 years, and the efficiency decreases with age. Scientists think that the solar panels on cars will deteriorate even quicker due to the jolting about experienced on the road.

What is the biggest problem in solar technology?

The solar-powered "Stella" from Australia

Solar Car Races

While solar cars have yet to become a realistic option for the ordinary driver, solar enthusiasts have been racing their experimental designs since the 1980s.

The World Solar Challenge started in 1983 and takes place every three years. Drivers race their solar vehicles more than 1,800 miles (3,000 km) across the Australian Outback. The Toyota American Solar Challenge is a similar race that takes place in North America, between Dallas, Texas, and Alberta, Canada.

CHAPTER 8
Hydrogen Power

Automobile manufacturers are constantly exploring new sources of fuel to power their cars. One exciting development is hydrogen—the most abundant element in the universe. Many experts think that hydrogen is the power of the future.

Early Invention

Hydrogen power may seem like a new idea, but the technology has been around since the middle of the 19th century—long before automobiles were invented. In 1842, British scientist Sir William Grove demonstrated that he could generate electricity by combining hydrogen and oxygen. This process takes place inside a type of battery called a fuel cell.

Today, engineers use hydrogen fuel cells to power electric motors in cars. Unlike fossil fuels, hydrogen does not produce harmful pollution. In fact, the only thing you will see coming out of the tailpipe of a hydrogen car is steam.

In 1842, Sir William Grove demonstrated that he could generate electricity by combining which two elements?

Fuel cells

William Grove's fuel cell is the powerhouse of today's hydrogen cars. He used a process called **electrolysis** to convert hydrogen gas and oxygen gas into water, producing electricity in the process. Grove named his invention the gas voltaic battery. We now call it the hydrogen fuel cell.

The fuel cell works by a simple chemical reaction between hydrogen and oxygen. Inside the fuel cell, the fuel—in this case, hydrogen—combines with oxygen gas taken from the air. Together, hydrogen and oxygen form water. Since the reaction produces a lot of heat, the water is given off in its gas form—steam.

Concept Cars

It took a long time to develop hydrogen as a fuel for transportation. In the 1960s, fuel cells were developed to power spacecraft. The first hydrogen-powered buses appeared in the late 1990s. More recently, car manufacturers such as BMW, Chevrolet, and Honda have designed concept cars using hydrogen power.

In a hydrogen-powered car, the hydrogen is stored inside a fuel tank, while oxygen is taken from the air. A pump delivers the hydrogen to a stack of fuel cells, where it reacts with oxygen to form electricity and steam. The electricity goes directly to the motor to turn the wheels of the car. Any extra electricity is stored inside a battery to be used later. The steam passes out of the car's exhaust system.

Hydrogen is the cleanest, lightest, and most abundant power source discovered so far. Could it be the solution for eco-friendly cars of the future?

The fuel tank contains compressed hydrogen gas instead of gasoline. The tank needs to be strong because the hydrogen is highly explosive.

Capacitors store the electricity that powers the electric motor to drive the wheels.

The exhaust pipe emits steam instead of harmful gases such as carbon dioxide.

94

The LIFEcar

- Designed by the Morgan Motor Company

- Unveiled at the Geneva Motor Show in 2008

- Car body made from aluminum sheets

- Electric motor powered by hydrogen

- 0-60 mph (0-96 km/h) in 7 seconds

- Energy efficiency 150 miles (241 km) per gallon

- Zero emissions

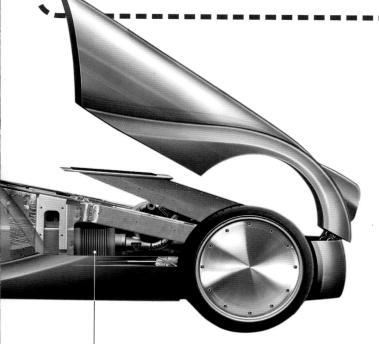

The fuel cells are stacked up in layers to produce more electricity to power the car.

Hydrogen advantages

Hydrogen power is still in the early stages of development. Hydrogen fuel cells are efficient and reliable, and the only waste product from them is harmless steam. But there are also many challenges that need to be overcome.

Hydrogen disadvantages

Fuel cells use an expensive metal called platinum to drive the reaction between hydrogen and oxygen, making the cost of hydrogen cars too expensive for most people.

Another problem is how to refuel

these cars. Where would you fill up your tank with hydrogen gas? It would take time and a lot of money to build a network of hydrogen refueling stations.

Storing the hydrogen onboard the car is also an issue. Hydrogen is a very light gas and it is difficult to squeeze the hydrogen into a tank small enough to fit inside a car. Hydrogen is also extremely explosive. A leaking tank could explode, so the hydrogen fuel needs to be stored safely.

The final problem is exactly how environmentally friendly hydrogen cars might be. Hydrogen is collected from water using electricity, which usually comes from power stations that burn coal and other fossil fuels.

It may take another 20 to 30 years before hydrogen power becomes a commercial reality.

CARS OF THE FUTURE

Engineers are constantly developing ideas for new vehicles and new forms of eco-friendly energy instead of gasoline. Will you drive one of these vehicles in the future?

The electric Toyota i-Road combines the size of a motorcycle with the comfort of a car.

The Solomon Fuel Cell Vehicle runs on hydrogen. Reduced leakage means improved safety.

The Audi Urban has two electric motors powered by a lithium-ion battery pack.

CHAPTER 9
Racing Machines

Car manufacturers are always pushing the limits of technology to build faster cars with more powerful engines. It is no surprise that some people like to drive these speed machines in competitive races. Indeed, motor racing in its many different forms continues to be one of the most popular sports in the world.

History of Motorsport

The first motor races took place in Europe at the end of the 19th century. These races often took place on open roads. The first real motor race was a 730-mile (1,168-km) route in France, from Paris to Bordeaux and back again. It took the winning French driver Emile Levassor nearly 49 hours to complete.

Motor racing in the United States started with the Chicago Times-Herald race in 1895. The race covered several laps of a 55-mile (88-km) course around the south side of Chicago and was won by American driver Frank Duryea.

The first racetrack built specifically for motor racing was Brooklands, which opened in Great Britain in 1907. This circuit closed in 1939 due to the start of World War II, because it was needed as a base for building aircraft.

The oldest racetrack in the United States is the Indianapolis Motor Speedway, which opened in 1909. Today, this circuit is one of the biggest sporting venues in the world, with space for more than 250,000 spectators.

Different forms of motor sport emerged in the 20th century, from Formula One (F1) to stock car racing. The governing body for all motor racing is the Fédération Internationale de l'Automobile (FIA). The FIA decides the rules of racing, the power of race cars, the design of the racetracks, and the safety of drivers and spectators.

Formula One

The fastest motor sport, using the most powerful motor cars, is Formula One or F1. The F1 races, called Grand Prix, are held on circuits all over the world, from the streets of Monaco in Europe to the Circuit of the Americas in Austin, Texas. F1 cars can accelerate to speeds of up to 220 miles (360 km) per hour on straight sections of the circuit.

As the winner crosses the finishing line, a race official waves a black-and-white checkered flag. Drivers win points for each Grand Prix. At the end of the season, the driver with the most points is crowned World Champion.

NASCAR

A popular form of motorsport in the United States is stock car racing. This sport is governed by NASCAR, which stands for the National Association for Stock Car Auto Racing. Stock car racing traces its origins back to the middle of the 20th century, when a US mechanic, William France, began to promote the sport in Daytona Beach in Florida.

Over the years, stock car racing has expanded into many different forms. The Sprint Cup Series includes the most prestigious race, the Daytona 500, a 500-mile (800-km) race held at the Daytona International Speedway in Florida. This race attracts millions of TV spectators around the world.

Indy Car

IndyCar racing is also popular in the United States. IndyCar racing uses open-wheeled cars, with the wheels outside the main body of the car so that the race cars look similar to F1 cars.

Like all forms of motor racing, strict rules govern the specifications of the cars used in the races, which take place on circuits across the United States, including street courses. The Indianapolis 500 is the most prestigious IndyCar Series race. This 500-mile race takes place on the Indianapolis Motor Speedway in Indiana.

Indy 500 race car, 1978

Moto Racing

Not all motorsport takes place on four wheels. Moto racing is the name given to a wide range of motorcycle racing, which includes road races, motocross, and track racing.

The motorcycle equivalent of F1 racing is called the Motorcycle Grand Prix or MotoGP for short, which is a series of 18 race meetings on circuits in 13 countries around the world. At each meeting, riders compete in three different World Championship Grand Prix categories. Each category uses motorcycles with different specifications. The highest class involves racing powerful four-stroke 1,000cc motorcycles that are specially designed for professional racing.

Other popular forms of motorcycle competitions include motocross, the off-road equivalent to road racing. Motocross takes place on a variety of surfaces, from dirt and grass to sand and mud.

Speedway is another form of moto racing around laps of a flat dirt track using bikes with no brakes. Riders slow down by sliding the bikes sideways as they approach turns in the track.

Motocross racer jumping during a race

Other Motorsports

Many other kinds of motor races now take place. Rally racing takes place on open roads using normal cars with special modifications to make them faster. Rallying involves two people racing the rally car between set points.

One person drives the car and the other person navigates the route.

Rallying is one of the oldest forms of motorsport and has its origins in some of the earliest races, such as the Paris-Bordeaux-Paris race of 1895.

Do you want to be a race car driver?

Many race car drivers start by racing go-karts as children. These low-lying vehicles hug the track and give drivers the experience of racing, handling turns, and overtaking other vehicles.

As drivers become more skilled, they move to bigger, more powerful models. These off-road vehicles range from Bambino karts, designed to give young racers their first taste of karting, to racing buggies, which can accelerate from 0 to 60 mph (0-96 km/h) in under three seconds.

Racers first prove themselves on local tracks and then move up the ranks. The aim is to be noticed by a sponsor who will hire you to race their car professionally. It takes skill, luck, and a lot of practice.

RECORD BREAKERS

American Irvin Gordon has driven his Volvo P-1800S a staggering 2,966,000 miles (4,773,314 km) since he first bought it in 1966.

British driver **Andy Green** holds the land speed record for a car. In 1997, Green drove his *Thrust SSC* an incredible 763 mph (1,228 km/h).

Green also holds the land speed record for a diesel-powered car, the *JCB Dieselmax*, which reached a top speed of 350 mph (563 km/h) in 2006.

At age 21, German **Sebastian Vettel** became the youngest driver to win a Formula 1 race at the 2008 Grand Prix circuit in Monza, Italy.

John McGuinness rode the fastest lap of the Isle of Man TT motorcycle race in 2009. He rode the 37-mile (59.5 km) lap in 17 minutes, 12.3 seconds on a Honda CBR1000RR.

The fastest electric car is the *Buckeye Bullet 2*, driven by American **Roger Schroder** at 308 mph (496 km/h) in 2010.

The world's fastest motorcycle, the *Top Oil-Ack Attack* streamliner, reached a speed of 376 mph (605 km/h) in 2010.

The fastest solar-powered vehicle, the *Sunswift IV*, reached a speed of 55 mph (89 km/h) on the flat deserts of Australia in 2011.

Croatians **Marko Tomac** and **Ivan Cvetković** hold the record for the longest trip on a single tank of fuel. In 2011, they drove 1,582 miles (2,546 km) without refueling in a diesel Volkswagen Passat 1.6 TDI BlueMotion.

The world's fastest electric-powered motorcycle is the SWIGZ Electric Superbike Prototype, ridden by American **Chip Yates** at a speed of 197 mph (317 km/h) on the Bonneville Salt Flats in Utah in 2011.

Swiss couple **Emil** and **Liliana Schmid** hold the record for the longest car trip. Between 1984 and 2014, they covered more than 430,050 miles (692,098 km) in their Toyota Land Cruiser.

The most successful NASCAR drivers are Americans **Richard Petty** and **Dale Earnhardt** who have both recorded seven Sprint Cup Series Drivers' Championships.

The world's fastest road race is the Silver State Classic in Nevada, where average speeds on the 90-mile (145 km) course of straight, flat roads reach more than 190 mph (306 km/h).

113

CHAPTER 10
The Future

The short-term future of motor cars is affected by the main concern about the use of fossil fuels. Scientists and engineers are looking to develop environmentally friendly fuels such as hydrogen power and make them affordable for all motorists. Other developments may seem like science fiction, but these dreams could turn into reality and revolutionize the way we drive in the future.

Driverless Cars

One exciting vision for the future of motoring is driverless cars. In 2010, the American car manufacturer General Motors released a driverless car called the Electric Networked-Vehicle (EN-V). The EN-V is an electric car that can travel at speeds of up to 25 miles (40 km) an hour. It is designed to be used for short trips in congested city centers.

One of the most exciting features of the EN-V is that it does not need a driver. Instead, computers will control the car and use WiFi signals to stay in touch with other EN-V cars on the road. Sensors on the car will ensure that the vehicles do not collide.

How will the Electric Networked-Vehicle (EN-V) operate without a driver? How can it ensure that the vehicles do not collide?

The computer and technology company Google has tested similar self-driving cars on the highways of California and Nevada. Google's cars record images of the road as they drive to "learn" commonly taken routes and rely on computer maps to navigate to the destination. Google has also employed laser and radar technologies to ensure safety on the road. Google's self-drive cars use these technologies to identify pedestrians on the road and automatically stop to allow them to cross. Google has also addressed the problem of congestion (traffic jams) by "platooning." In this process, the Google cars drive very close to each other, acting like a "train" of cars. Google believes that platooning will reduce congestion and prevent accidents caused by annoyed and frustrated drivers.

Interactive Cars

Another new technology is called Vehicle-to-Vehicle (V2V) communication. Manufacturers such as Ford are developing V2V with the aim of reducing the number of traffic accidents. V2V could prevent collisions by sending WiFi signals to any nearby vehicles. These signals keep cars at a safe distance from each other and could even be designed to slam on the brakes if the system detects the likelihood of a collision.

Engineers have developed the idea of V2V communication even further with vehicle-to-infrastructure (V2I) communication. This could allow cars on the road to interact with road and traffic signals. V2I could even be used to provide cars with information about traffic on the road, so the car could automatically reroute and find a quicker way to get to the destination.

Augmented Reality

Another development of the future is the Augmented Reality (AR) display. Many modern automobiles have computerized dashboards with Global Positioning Satellite (GPS) navigation to give drivers information about traffic and road conditions. AR displays take this technology a step further by presenting the information on the windshield.

The AR display would show the driver information on top of what he or she is seeing in real life. If the driver gets too close to the car in front, the AR display would shine a red warning symbol on the windshield to warn of the impending danger. Augmented Reality displays could combine with GPS systems to inform the driver of traffic congestion and suggest an alternative route in front of his or her eyes.

Safety Systems

Car manufacturers take safety very seriously. They are developing new systems to make driving safer than ever. One new idea being developed by Mercedes-Benz is to extend the use of passenger airbags into "car airbags" to stop the vehicles before they crash. The system uses sensors to detect a collision before it happens. If the collision seems likely, airbags would be deployed underneath the car to bring it to a safe stop.

How would car airbags stop a vehicle before it crashes?

Make a **Magnetic Car**

Make a car powered by magnets! It works because two magnets can either attract or repel each other when they are brought close together. The magnets will either push or pull your car, depending on which ends of the magnets are facing each other.

You will need:

two bar magnets

empty matchbox

compass

modeling clay

tape

card

two toothpicks

scissors

drinking straw

1 Tape one of the magnets into the tray of the matchbox. Slide the tray back into the matchbox.

2 Cut two pieces of the straw the same size as the shorter side of the matchbox.

3 Tape the pieces of straw to the outside of the matchbox.

4 Use the compass to draw four equal circles on the card. Carefully cut them out. These are the wheels.

5 Push the toothpicks through the straws. Use clay to attach the wheels to the toothpicks.

6 Place the matchbox car on a flat surface. Bring the other magnet close. The car will roll either toward the magnet or away from it.

Turn the magnet around and the car will roll in the other direction.

FAST AND COOL CARS QUIZ

See if you can find the answers to these questions about what you have read.

1. In which year did Karl Benz make the first four-wheeled car?

2. How many pistons are in a V12 engine?

3. What was the nickname of the Ford Model T?

4. What does combustion mean?

5. Hybrid cars combine gasoline power with what other form of energy?

6. What is the top speed of the Harley Davidson "Fat Boy"?

7. Which engine part converts the up-and-down movement of the pistons into the circular movement of the wheels?

8. What are the top two countries with the largest oil reserves?

9. Who made the first two-wheeled motorcycle?

10. What was the name of the first solar-powered car?

11. Why does a hydrogen fuel tank need to be strong?

12. What is the raw material used to produce gasoline?

13. Why is burning fossil fuels bad for the planet?

14. What does NASCAR stand for?

15. How does V2V prevent collisions?

Answers on page 125.

GLOSSARY

Battery
Device that changes the energy in chemicals into electricity.

Carburetor
Device that mixes air wth a fine spray of fuel in an internal-combustion engine.

Crankshaft
Engine part that converts the up-and-down movement of the pistons into the rotation of the wheels.

Cylinder
Metal tube inside an engine in which fuel is burned to produce heat energy.

Efficiency
Working to achieve the best and be the most useful.

Electric motor
Machine that converts electricity into movement.

Electrolysis
Process using electricity to break down chemicals into simpler substances.

Emissions
Sending out something such as a gas in a car's exhaust.

Fossil fuels
Fuels, such as coal or gas, formed from the remains of animals and plants that lived millions of years ago.

Fuel cell
Battery combining hydrogen gas with oxygen to produce electricity.

Internal combustion engine
Engine that burns fuel in a closed chamber to generate power.

Pollution
Harmful substances in the environment.

Prototype
First working model of a machine.

Regenerative brakes
Technology in hybrid cars in which energy produced when the car brakes generates electricity to charge the battery.

Semiconductor
A solid substance that electricity can pass through in some conditions but not others.

Supercharger
A device that increases the flow of air into an internal combustion engine to boost its power.

Suspension
System of springs and shock absorbers that support a vehicle on its wheels, so the drive is not so bumpy.

Transmission
System of transferring the power from an engine to the wheels' axle in a motor vehicle.

Answers to the Fast and Cool Cars Quiz:
1. 1893; **2.** 12; **3.** Tin Lizzie; **4.** Burning; **5.** Electricity; **6.** 110 miles (177 km) per hour; **7.** Crankshaft; **8.** Venezuela and zbia; **9.** Gottlieb Daimler; **10.** Bluebird; **11.** Hydrogen is highly explosive so the tank must not get damaged; **12.** Crude oil; **13.** It creates pollution; **14.** National Association for Stock Car Auto Racing; **15.** Sends WiFi signals to any nearby vehicles.

INDEX

About the Author

My name is Leon Gray, and I live in a small village called Kemnay near Aberdeen in the northeast of Scotland. When I was at school, I liked to read books about science, so I went to University College, London, to study zoology (the science of animals). After graduating in 1995, I started working for a publishing company in London. Since then, I have written and edited more than 100 books for young readers just like you—mainly about science, technology, and the natural world. I hope that reading this book inspires you to start writing about topics that interest you!

About the Consultant

Dr. Linda Gambrell, Distinguished Professor of Education at Clemson University, has served as President of the National Reading Conference, the College Reading Association, and the International Reading Association. She is also reading consultant to the *DK Readers*.

Have you read these other great books from DK?

DK ADVENTURES

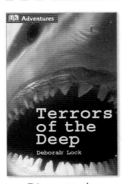

Discover the wonders of the world's deepest, darkest ocean trench.

Experience ancient Roman intrigue in this time-traveling adventure.

Encounter the rare animals in the mountain forests of Cambodia.

Time-travel to the Wild West and get caught up in fossil hunters' rivalry.

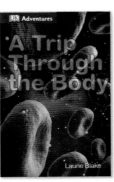

Explore the amazing systems at work inside the human body.

Step back nearly 20,000 years to the days of early cave dwellers.